F*ck I'm Bored!

#2

Activity Book For Adults

Featuring 100 Adult Activities Such As: Word Searches, Dot-to-Dot, Mazes, Fallen Phrases, Math Logic, Spot the Difference, Word Tiles, Word Scramble, Cryptogram, Sudoku, Draw the Squares, Hidden Image and Games to Play with a friend.

Each page has a fun adult activity.

Thank you for your purchase!
I hope you enjoy the book.

Please consider leaving a review and checking out my
Amazon collection!

Contact me to get a free printable PDF of activities at:
http://www.tamaraladamsauthor.com/free-printable-activity-book-pdf/

http://www.amazon.com/T.L.-Adams/e/B00YSROGC4

tamaraadamsauthor@gmail.com

www.tamaraladamsauthor.com

https://twitter.com/@TamaraLAdams

https://www.facebook.com/TamaraLAdamsAuthor/

https://www.pinterest.com/tamara-l-adams-author/

All Cartoon Drawings are from https://publicdomainvectors.org

Don't be a jerk or a bully. It's rude.
Start at the top and work your way down.

Answer on page 101

There are probably many things that we do that really make people assholes, but for now find the 10 bananas that have been hidden in the image below.

Answer on page 101

Connect the dots from 100 to 143 to find that Shit. Don't let the extra numbers fool you!

230 278 240
258 268 248 249 245 244 238
218 264 233 233 276 243
223 246 264 253 242 257
238 246 245 247 250 237 237 259
251 254 243 250 237 272 170
257 254 255 255 274 166 171 239
238 270 279 236
104 145 105 226 254 185 275 119 262 271
271 248 249
144 214 258 236 168 167 121 269
262 265 230 106 110 116 117 169 210
256 103 102 250 115 243 272 120 197 265
101 241 239 212 247 122 266 267
242 146 241 112 241
244 259 239 107 109 114 118 123 269
253 108 111 113
239 100 222 211 195 172 268 260 277
237 237 239 196 250
147 236 261 174 188 245 263
236 259 226 256 184
268 225 275 263
235 125 124 133 132 142 143
212 198 238 175 173
217 210 131 134 141 176 240
235 271 126 135 139 140 206
279 209 207 276 278 178 177
239 213 130 236 236 261 248 187
127 189 199 201 186 179
266 215 214 273 181 182 180
234 238 128 129 137 269 138 183
260 228 278 217 215 260 194 213
263 266 276 264 200 273 275 249
251 231 218 267 237
277 220 256 216 209 193
270 261 270 274 246 252
262 279 265 227 247 208 252
238 237 228 229 224 202 274
234 224 242 225 190 151 251
252 244 192
272 216 253 227 191 211
267 257 258 231
204 273 148 255 205
229

Answer on page 101

3

A fallen phrase puzzle is a shit puzzle where all the letters have fallen to the bottom. They got mixed up on their way down, but remain in the same damn row. Complete the fucked puzzle by filling the letters into the column they fall under. You start by filling in the one-letter columns (easy as fuck), because those don't have anywhere else to go in their column.
Also try filling in common one-, two- and three-letter words as shown in the example below.

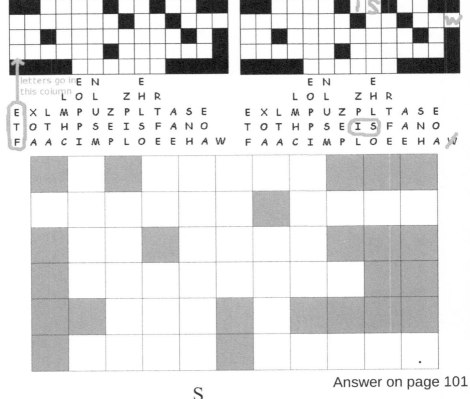

letters go in this column

E   N   E
   L O L   Z H R
E X L M P U Z P L T A S E
T O T H P S E I S F A N O
F A A C I M P L O E E H A W

E   N   E
   L O L   Z H R
E X L M P U Z P L T A S E
T O T H P S E I S F A N O
F A A C I M P L O E E H A W

Answer on page 101

S

J W L A   I P
S O U L R C U
T B S T I O N N
I U T T T I D A R
R E A E R Y E H G T D

Math Squares

Somebody fucked shit up with this puzzle.
Try to fill in the missing numbers if you damn well can.

Use the numbers 1 through 9 to complete the equations.

Each row is a goddamn math equation. Work your way from left to right. And don't fucking cheat.

But that's not all, bitch! Each column is it's own shit math equation. Work that shit from top to bottom.

What kind of annoying things do you do in public?

9	/		+	4	7
-		X		/	
	-	8	X		-2
+		/		+	
5	-		X	1	-1

7	4	3

Answer on page 101

Color this shit and add your own doodles.

What do you do for others so you're not a dick?
Fit the numbered bricks into the square of bricks
without changing their shape or breaking them up.

8	8	8

1	1	1
	1	

4	4	4
	4	4

2		
2	2	
2	2	2

7	7
	7

| 6 | | |
| 6 | 6 | 6 |

5	5	5
5	5	5

3		3
3	3	3

Answer on page 101

Try not to be a racist asshole. Answer on page 101

You are given this crap piece of text where each letter is substituted with a number and you need to goddamn decide which letters in the alphabet are being coded by the numbers you are given. Example is given here:

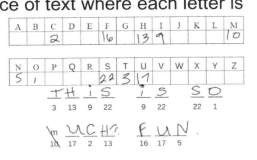

A	B	C	D	E	F	G	H	I	J	K	L	M
		2			16		13	9				10

N	O	P	Q	R	S	T	U	V	W	X	Y	Z
5	1				22	3	17					

THiS   iS   SO
3 13 9 22   9 22   22 1

MUCH?   FUN.
10 17 2 13   16 17 5

A	B	C	D	E	F	G	H	I
					3			

J	K	L	M	N	O	P	Q	R

S	T	U	V	W	X	Y	Z

___ ' ___   ___ ___ ___ ___ ___ ___
7   22   18 1   9 14 14 24

___ ___   f ___ ___ ___ ___ ,
 9 14   3 21 18 15

___ ___ ___   ___   ___ ___ ___ ___
 4 21   5   7   18 21 14 14

___   ___ ___ ___ ___ ___ ___ .
 9   1   7   5   5   1 17

What do you think people do that's so uncool? Find the one prick below that matches the asshole bastard shadow here on the left

Answer on page 101

A B  C 
D  E  F 
G  H  I 
J  K  L 
M  N  O 
P  Q  R

Please don't be rude in public, no one likes it.

The figures given on the side and in top of the grid indicate the numbers of black boxes in that line or column.

For example 3,3 on the left of a line indicates that there is, from left to right, a block of 3 black boxes then a second damn block of 3 black boxes on the same shite line.
To solve a puzzle, one needs to determine which cells will be boxes and which will be empty. Determining which cells are to be left empty is as important as those to be filled.

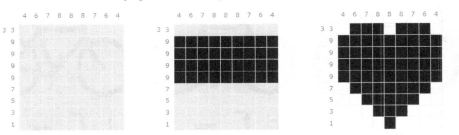

Answer on page 101

	4, 1	1, 1, 1	1, 4	0	7	1	7	0	1, 1	7	1, 1	0	1	7	1
3, 1, 1, 3, 3															
1, 1, 1, 1, 1															
1, 1, 1, 1, 1															
3, 3, 1, 1															
1, 1, 1, 1, 1															
1, 1, 1, 1, 1															
3, 1, 1, 3, 1															

This is probably how you feel every damn day.
Find the 10 differences between the two images

Answer on page 102

Number Blocks

Try to fill in all the bastard missing numbers.

The missing numbers are integers from 1 to 9.
The numbers in each row add up to totals to the right.
The numbers in each column add up to the totals along the bottom. I know it's a lot but it's better than work!
The diagonal lines also add up the totals to the right.

Also, stop fishing for compliments, no one wants to tell you that you are amazing all the fucking time!

				26
3		6	5	15
4	2			23
	7		2	20
5		1		17
20	14	19	22	15

Answer on page 102

Don't leave vague posts on social media. No one gives a fuck! Unscramble all of these shit phrases.

1. uFsng ickthi   _____

2. oha inf ob Stc   _____

3. guaFcr etgnki   _____

4. heaoC tfccr   _____

5. lfkc emy Fiu   _____

6. rcsohke stcWol _____

7. zfichi stut tobzfB _____

8. as ksoY su cu   _____

9. eahy tp oifs eLizc _____

10. fosf isP   _____

11. Ge hoo tll   _____

12. Usp uyro   _____

Answer on page 102

Letter Tiles

I can't understand what the fuck any of this says.
Try to have some fucking fun moving all the damn tiles
around to make the correct stupich phrase. The three
letters on each tile must stay together and in the given
order. Cheating won't help your ass with this one.

J A R	C K I	C O	F U	S W E
C E		F I	P R O	C E	M .
T H E	G R A	M Y	N G	U L D
A R	S P A	N A N		

M Y				

Answer on page 102

Don't talk about shit you know nothing about

Peckerhead   shitbag   bugger   twat
Dingkeberry   nutsack   blimey   git
Fucknugget   wanker   jackoff   dildo

Answer on page 102

What the shit is this? Draw the damn squares.

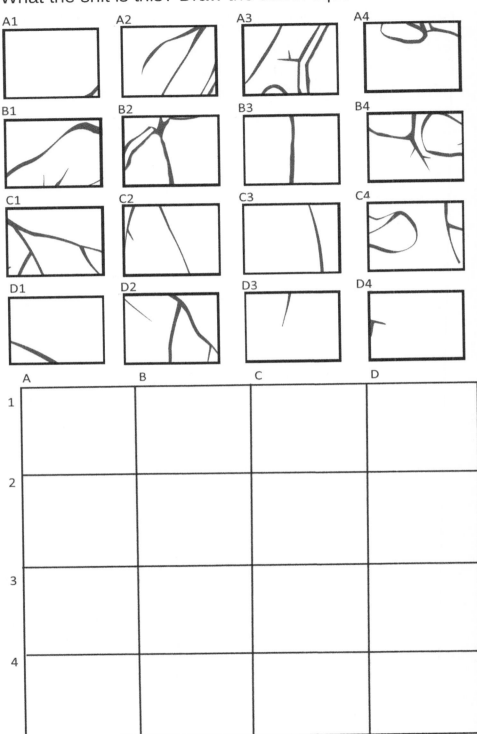

Image on page 102

Do you put your cart away, Bitch? Find the different 1

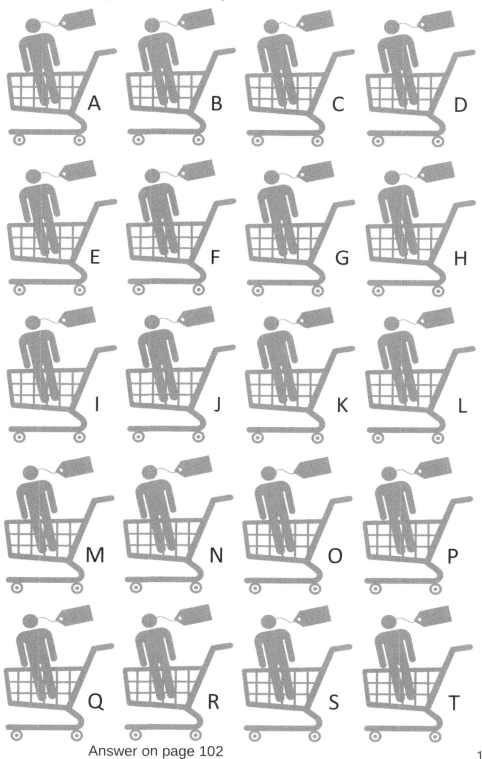

Answer on page 102

Never bully or yell at others, it's damn rude.
How many crazy dots can you find in the image below?

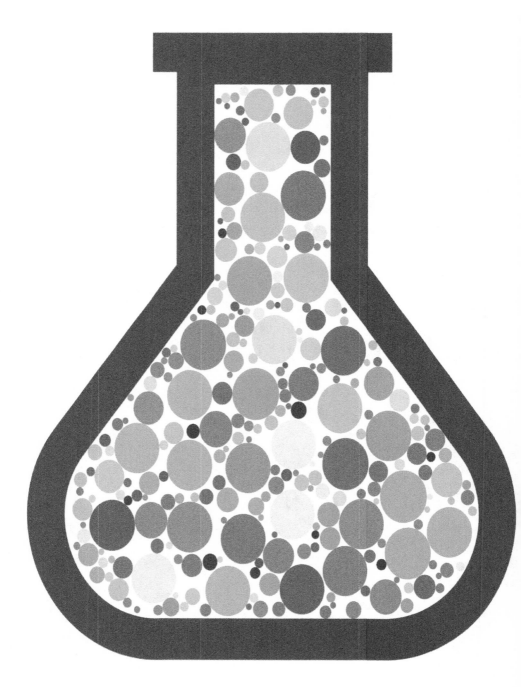

Answer on page 103

OMG what the shit is this? Too many numbers if you ask me! Your task is to fill every empty cell with a positive or negative integer in such a way so that each white cell's value equals the sum of its adjoining half-height cells. When complete, each Balance Quest puzzle grid will "balance" itself in such a way so that the four center cells surrounding the center "zero cell" will always add up to zero.

There are five rules that must be followed in every Quest puzzle:
The gray cells must include all integers between -16 and 16, except 0
No number can be repeated within any of the gray cells.
The number in each white cell must equal the sum of its adjoining cells. The center Zero cell is always the sum of all four adjacent cells.

** Numbers can (and will) be reused across both white and gray cells. The rules specify only that the -16 to 16 numbers can never be used more than once in the gray cells. Example is below:

<table>
<tr><td>-8</td><td rowspan="2">-2</td></tr>
<tr><td>6</td></tr>
<tr><td>5</td><td rowspan="2">4</td></tr>
<tr><td>-1</td></tr>
</table>

-8+6=-2
-1+5=4

<table>
<tr><td>-2</td><td rowspan="2">2</td></tr>
<tr><td>4</td></tr>
</table>

-2+4=-2

<table>
<tr><td>2</td><td rowspan="2">0</td><td>-1</td></tr>
<tr><td>-9</td><td>8</td></tr>
</table>

2+-9+
-1+8=0

<table>
<tr><td></td><td rowspan="2">4</td><td rowspan="4">-2</td><td rowspan="8"></td><td rowspan="16">0</td><td rowspan="8">-33</td><td rowspan="4"></td><td rowspan="2">4</td><td></td></tr>
<tr><td>-8</td><td>-7</td></tr>
<tr><td>13</td><td rowspan="2"></td><td rowspan="2"></td><td>-13</td></tr>
<tr><td></td><td></td></tr>
<tr><td>-9</td><td rowspan="2"></td><td rowspan="4"></td><td rowspan="4">-29</td><td rowspan="2"></td><td>10</td></tr>
<tr><td></td><td></td></tr>
<tr><td></td><td rowspan="2">-10</td><td rowspan="2">3</td><td>-6</td></tr>
<tr><td>-16</td><td></td></tr>
<tr><td>-2</td><td rowspan="2">13</td><td rowspan="4">5</td><td rowspan="8">11</td><td rowspan="8"></td><td rowspan="4"></td><td rowspan="2"></td><td></td></tr>
<tr><td></td><td>4</td></tr>
<tr><td>-10</td><td rowspan="2"></td><td rowspan="2">-27</td><td>-12</td></tr>
<tr><td></td><td></td></tr>
<tr><td>16</td><td rowspan="2"></td><td rowspan="4"></td><td rowspan="4">2</td><td rowspan="2"></td><td></td></tr>
<tr><td></td><td>3</td></tr>
<tr><td>-11</td><td rowspan="2">-12</td><td rowspan="2">-9</td><td></td></tr>
<tr><td></td><td>-5</td></tr>
</table>

Answer on page 103

Who the fuck left this shit this way. Bunch of dumbasses. Fix this damn thing.

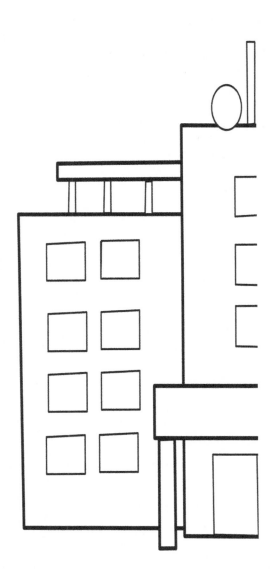

You're a dick if you self checkout with too many items.

Numbers from 1 to 9 are inserted into sets that have 9 x 9 = 81 squares in whole. Every number can be used just goddamn once in every, 3x3 block, column and row.

- Every number can be used just once in the blocks of 3 x 3 = 9 square blocks. Got that shit?
- Each row of 9 numbers ought to contain all digits 1 through 9 in any order. So don't leave a damn one out.
- Every column of 9 numbers should comprise all digits 1 through 9 in any order also.

One way to figure out which numbers can go in each space is to use "process of elimination" by checking to see which other numbers are already included within each square – since there can be no duplication of numbers 1-9 within each square (or row or column).

					9			6
					3	8	5	1
	6	2		1	5			
		7					6	
	2	1	9	7	6	3	8	
		3				1		
			4	5		9	7	
2	5	8	6					
4			3					

Answer on page 103

How many words can you find within the phrase:

Stop fucking shit up already

1._____
2._____
3._____
4._____
5._____
6._____
7._____
8._____
9._____
10._____
11._____
12._____
13._____
14._____
15._____
16._____
17._____
18._____
19._____
20._____
21._____
22._____
23._____
24._____
25._____

This is a bunch of fucked up math but go ahead and try to give that shit a try.

For this fucking bitch of a problem use only the numbers 1, 2 and 3 to solve all the shit issues in the box.
The numbers in each heavily outlined set of squares, called cages, must combine (in any order) to produce the target number in the top corner using the mathematical operation indicated (+, -, ×, ÷). Use each number only once per row, once per column. Cages with just one square should be filled in with the target number in the top corner. A number can be repeated within a cage as long as it is not in the same row or column. Did you get all that crap? Good luck!

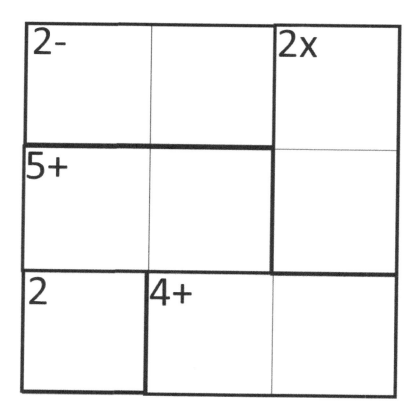

Answer on page 103

Only assholes brag about themselves all the time.
Players take turns in naming a letter. As each letter is named each player must write it immediately into one of the cells in their own grid. Players can choose any letter they like, and letters can be repeated. When the grid is full the players count up the number of four-letter words they have made, reading across, down, or diagonally, and the one with the highest score wins. Tip: you can either choose letters to help you complete words, or you can fuck up your opponent's words.

This player earns 6 points with these words: CARD, TOSS, COAT, RIPS, DOTS, and CUPS

C	A	R	D
O	U	I	O
A	B	P	T
T	O	S	S

This player wins with 7 points from these words: CARP, AUTO, CATS, SOBS, PODS, POTS, STOP

C	A	R	P
A	U	O	O
T	T	I	D
S	O	B	S

Take turns placing your mark (o or x) in a square in the grid. The first person to get three in a row wins. If all 9 squares are filled in before someone gets three in a row, the game ends in a fucked up tie.

Try and find the 11  cigarettes in the image, bitch.

Do you talk about yourself all the damn time!
Maybe try to stop. Solve this damn Maze already!

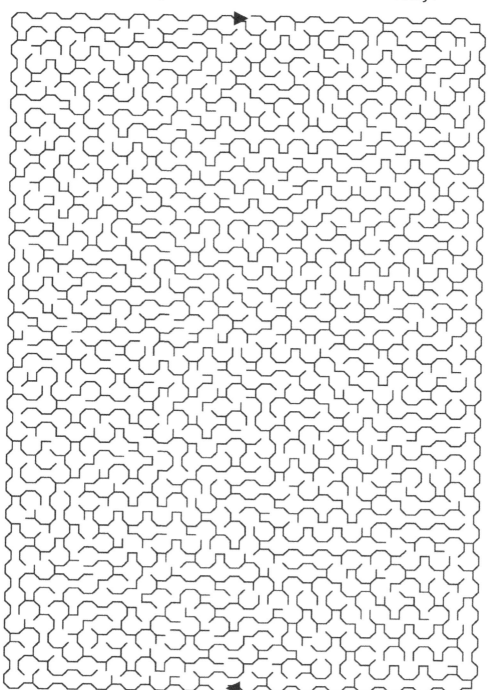

Answer on page 103

Connect the damn dots from 100 to 148
Don't let the extra numbers mess you up!

258   230   278   240   276   118
268   248   249   245   242   244   243
218   238   233   162
223   233   264   253   272   117   121
238   246   246   245   247   119   120
254   248   243   255   250   237   116   158
251   257   255   274   275   236   122
156   254   226   279   254   185   166   249   159
270   114   115   259   160   167   157
271   113   115   236   168   149   155
265   264   250   258   154   257   169   123   265
262   112   269   129   128   243   241   266
256   239   239   241   239   212   210   268
259   242   241   164   214   171   163   124   197
111   150   237   262   256   127   170   125   267
244   238   253   222   195   130   126   245   260
237   239   237   261   271   250
110   236   259   226   196   131   172   174   224   263
236   268   225   211   239   277   132   275   236   188   263   240
235   109   212   207   210   269   173   238   175   176
235   217   108   266   153   209   198   238   248   278   177
266   279   215   144   143   152   133   199   248   187   178   236
260   234   107   279   214   151   189   260   186   187   179
165   228   265   161   201   276   273   200   184   183   182   181   180
263   278   217   228   206   215   209   275   194   213
106   256   264   191   218   273   267   237   249   269
277   105   145   270   231   134   135   246   252   193
104   220   261   216   208   136   252
103   146   227   247   142   208   136
270   224   147   238   237   141   229   137   202   274   252
234   252   227   261   251
102   262   148   244   276   225   190   138   192   211
101   216   242   140   139   273   247   231   271
272   267   100   274   251   258   205   229   220
257   204   253   255

Answer on page 103

Cryptogram

Answer on page 103

You are given this crap piece of text where each letter is substituted with a number and you need to goddamn decide which letters in the alphabet are being coded by the numbers you are given. Example shown here:

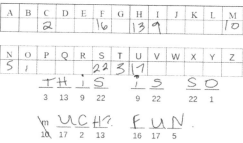

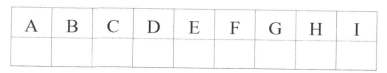

A	B	C	D	E	F	G	H	I

J	K	L	M	N	O	P	Q	R
								20

S	T	U	V	W	X	Y	Z

___   r   ___ ___ ___ ___ ___
9   20   25   22   13   13   24

___ ___ ___   '   ___   ___ ___ ___ ___
8   10   26   6   15   9   12   25

___ ___ ___   ___ ___ ___ ___ ___
6   7   10   23   19   9   6   23

___ ___ ___ ___ ___   ___ ___ ___   .
22   5   10   17   6   24   10   17

29

Pick up after your damn self! Find the one pussy below that matches the asshole bastard here on the left

Answer on page 104

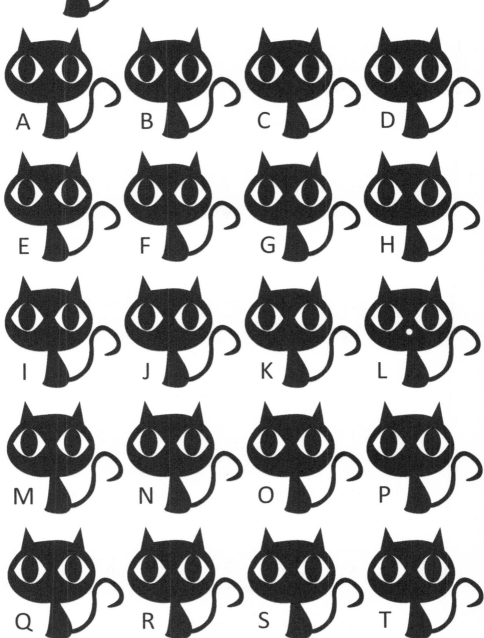

Stop complaining all the fucking time, it irritates others!

fucksville   prick   shitty   ballsack

dickweed   cock   asshat   buttmunch

shitkicker   dick   arsehole   shitfaced

```
                        E   D   N   L   T   Y   M
                        N   G   E   W   S   Z   O
                    Z   Q   F   X   I   O   P   Y   M
                    J   H   F   I   W   R   S   I   J
                    R   V   H   D   I   Q   W   F   H
                    V   P   M   C   B   S   X   P   L
                    R   Y   K   S   H   F   S   K   C
                    O   F   T   W   T   U   C   M   R
                    T   U   O   L   J   I   P   F   H
                    O   G   F   D   D   X   G   J   M
                    J   L   M   E   W   S   Z   U   V
                    W   S   H   I   T   T   Y   W   P
                    Z   K   B   K   B   S   S   A   H
                    J   W   T   U   Y   M   W   R   V
                    R   E   B   P   N   O   X   V   P
                    V   K   C   O   C   T   S   R   Y
                    R   Y   I   K   H   K   B   O   B
                    O   F   T   W   T   C   A   U   U
                    T   U   O   L   J   M   L   O   G
                    O   G   F   D   W   B   L   J   L
                    J   N   V   R   L   M   S   J   K
                    D   S   R   E   I   J   A   N   B
                    J   B   F   K   F   H   C   O   P
            E   S   X   V   J   U   P   C   P   L   K   W   X           J   O   P   S
        F   H   X   S   R   Y   C   H   F   I   V   C   H   J   K       O   F   P   F   H   X
    R   E   I   K   L   O   F   K   W   T   U   K   P   T   E   P   M   U   R   T   K   G   I   F   R
T   L   M   L   C   E   T   U   O   L   J   G   T   F   H   X   B   N   M   L   J   O   F   T   Y   T   G
V   S   T   A   H   S   S   A   K   D   W   X   I   J   M   B   V   X   Q   W   R   T   U   F   P   F   P
P   Y   I   J   M   B   S   V   C   O   P   T   H   U   N   D   N   E   R   C   U   N   T   A   E   P   D
Y   F   T   U   N   D   O   P   R   W   X   P   S   U   E   L   O   H   E   S   R   A   L   C   R   Y   O
F   U   O   U   O   P   P   W   H   J   K   E   O   G   F   V   P   M   B   H   X   W   B   E   O   F   U
U   G   F   G   F   V   G   J   K   B   F   R   J   L   M   H   D   I   K   B   K   B   S   D   P   U   C
G   L   M   L   M   R   Z   U   V   C   S   P   W   U   C   O   F   E   W   T   U   Y   M   N   B   D   H
L   U   V   U   V   O   B   O   L   L   O   C   K   N   A   C   E   B   E   B   P   N   O   I   U   T   E
U   G   F   U   C   K   S   V   I   L   L   E   U   M   N   B   D   H   M   W   P   B   T   X   E   O   S
Q   C   X   M   N   B   L   N   G   F   D   M   C   O   I   U   T   U   X   H   K   E   S   I   P   L   L
E   S   D   O   U   C   H   E   C   A   T   O   E   Y   M   P   C   D   B   V   X   C   X   B   H   M   E
    X   B   N   M   L   J   H   F   T   S   R   Y   I   J   B   C   O   Y   T   E   N   I   V   X   S
    B   V   X   Q   W   R   V   U                           P   F   H   I   Y   D   E   E
        T   E   S   X   V   B                               P   I   O   P   F   H
```

Answer on page 104

Somebody has to fix this shit and it ain't going to be me. Have some fucking fun moving all the damn tiles around to make the correct stupich phrase. The three letters on each tile must stay together and in the given order.
If you make a mistake, it's okay, own up and fix it.

B E C	B E	U C K	C A	C A U
S E :	C K I	W H Y N G		A U S
T T	S E	O .	I F	C U R
N A	W A N	N D	F U	E I
I	I N G			

W H Y			

Answer on page 104

Are you one of the too many assholes on this planet.
How many fucking humans can you find in the circle?

Answer on page 104

Math Squares

Hey wicked pisser, try to fill in the missing numbers.

Use the numbers 1 through 9 to complete the equations.

Each row is a math equation. Work your way from left to right and try not to fuck up the cunt math.
Each column is a math equation. Work from top to bottom, so you got that shit to figure out too. Lucky you!

Now, if you do not walk in a single file line on a crowded street, you're a jerk and you need to move your ass over.

	x	3	/		**2**
x		**+**		**+**	
2	**-**		**x**	**8**	**-24**
/		**-**		**/**	
	-	**9**	**+**		**-1**

8		**-1**		**2**

Answer on page 104

Fallen Phrase

Answer on page 104

This is a fucked puzzle where all the wanked letters have fallen to the bottom. They got mixed up on the way down, but remain in the same shit row.

You complete the puzzle by filling the letters into damn the column they fall under. You start by filling in the one-letter columns, because those assholes don't have anywhere else to go in their fucked column.

Also try filling in common one-, two- and three-letter words as shown in the bitchin example below.

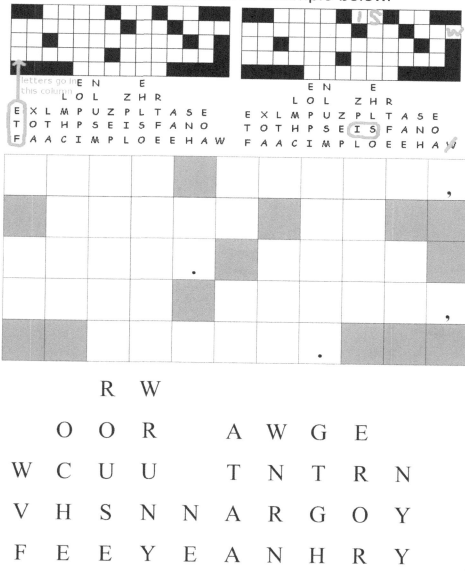

This shit is making me hungry.
Now draw the other half and color.

I'm not dealing with this shit, but you need to.
Fit the numbered bricks into the square of bricks
without changing their shape or breaking them up.

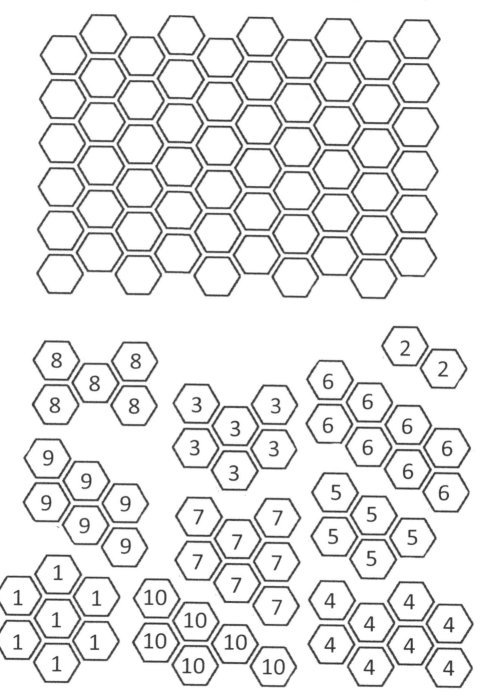

Answer on page 104

This is giving my a fucking anxiety attack!

Your task is to fill every empty cell with a positive or negative integer in such a way so that each white cell's value equals the sum of its adjoining half-height cells. When complete, each Balance Quest puzzle grid will "balance" itself in such a way so that the four center cells surrounding the center "zero cell" will always add up to zero.

There are five rules that must be followed in every Quest puzzle
The gray cells must include all integers between -16 and 16, except
No number can be repeated within any of the gray cells.
The number in each white cell must equal the sum of its adjoining cells. The center Zero cell is always the sum of all four adjacent cells

** Numbers can (and will) be reused across both white and gray cell
The rules specify only that the -16 to 16 numbers can never be used more than once in the gray cells. Example is below:

-8		-8+6=-2			-2+4=-2				2+-9+
	-2	-1+5=4	-2			2		-1	-1+8=0
6				2			0		
5									
	4		4			-9		8	
-1									

Answer on page 104

Color this shit! Your ass can do better.

GO TO HELL

I don't even know what this shit is! Draw the squares

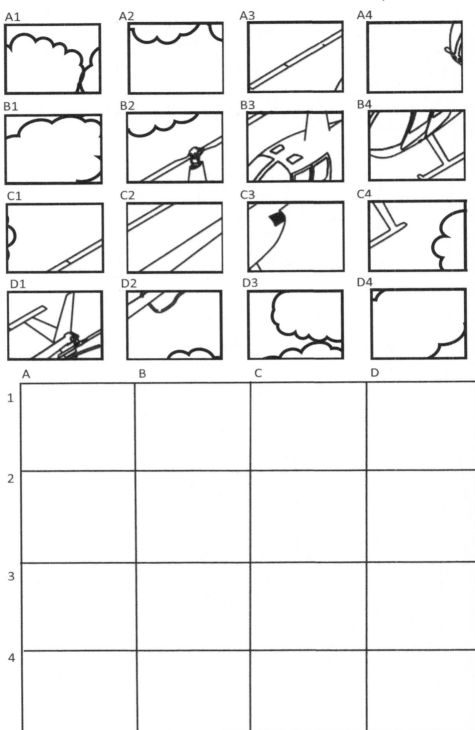

Image on page 104

Who the hell likes sudoku? Not my ass.

Numbers from 1 to 9 are inserted into sets that have 9 x 9 = 81 squares in whole. Every number can be used just goddamn once in every, 3x3 block, column and row.

- Every number can be used just once in the blocks of 3 x 3 = 9 square blocks. Got that shit?
- Each row of 9 numbers ought to contain all digits 1 through 9 in any order. So don't leave a damn one out.
- Every column of 9 numbers should comprise all digits 1 through 9 in any order also. Don't fuck it up.

One way to figure out which numbers can go in each space is to use "process of elimination" by checking to see which other numbers are already included within each square – since there can be no duplication of numbers 1-9 within each square (or row or column).

			5	1		8		2
				3	7			
6	5							9
		1	3		8			
9	8	4		7		1	5	3
			4		1	6		
2							8	4
		6	9					
3			5		8	2		

Answer on page 105

I can never figure this shit out but go ahead and try.

The figures given on the side and in top of the grid indicate the numbers of black boxes in that line or column.

For example 3,3 on the left of a line indicates that there is, from left to right, a block of 3 damn black boxes then a second block of 3 black boxes on the same crap line.
To solve a puzzle, one needs to determine which cells will be boxes and which will be empty. Determining which cells are to be left empty is as important as those to be filled.

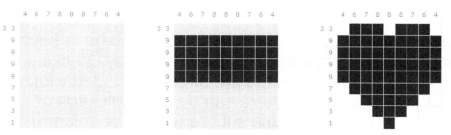

Answer on page 105

	4, 1	1, 1, 1	1, 4	0	7	1	7	0	1, 1	7	1, 1	0	1	7	1
3, 1, 1, 3, 3															
1, 1, 1, 1, 1															
1, 1, 1, 1, 1															
3, 3, 1, 1															
1, 1, 1, 1, 1															
1, 1, 1, 1, 1															
3, 1, 1, 3, 1															

Do not steal from others, it is super mean and rude.

For this problem use only the numbers 1, 2, 3 and 4 to solve. The numbers in each heavily outlined set of squares, called cages, must combine (in any order) to produce the target number in the top corner using the mathematical operation Indicated (+, -, ×, ÷). Is this shit fucked or what? Use each number only once per row, and also only fucking once per column. Cages with just one square should be filled in with the target number in the top corner. A number can be repeated within a cage as long as it is not in the same row or column. I'm lost too, but hey at least it's not work.

1-	6x		9+
	4	4÷	
1-	2x		
		4+	

Answer on page 105

These fucking monkeys are having a day. Find the 11 differences between the two images

Answer on page 105

Being late for everything is an asshole move.

Try to fill in some more damn missing numbers. Who the shit keeps losing these fuckers anyway.

The missing numbers are integers from 1 and 9.
The numbers in each row add up to totals to the right.
The numbers in each column add up to the totals along the bottom. You know the goddamn drill by now!
The diagonal lines also add up the totals to the right.

					20
8		2		1	20
	6		3	9	26
2		3	6		20
	7	5		2	27
6	9		3		30
21	27	22	26	27	33

Answer on page 105

Which one of these bitches is different from the rest?

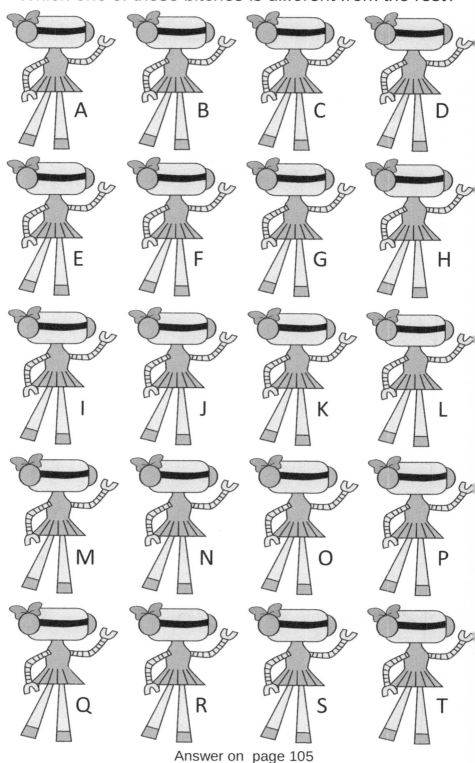

Answer on page 105

Unscramble the words about how you sound when you talk loud enough to make me deaf.

1. aad tsr tWabah   _____

2. dda ehE iat nits   _____

3. Lm ucic ytkn   _____

4. cn'b di ea Dotk   _____

5. rsAi sssek   _____

6. yhd ollBleo   _____

7. ihhut scs kFit   _____

8. eneP sfaci   _____

9. Soc kck cmuy   _____

10. Fcsuy ofrkelu   _____

11. yis mss Ksa   _____

12. tlers teo jkG   _____

Answer on page 105

How many words can you find within the words:

What the fuck are you doing

1._____
2._____
3._____
4._____
5._____
6._____
7._____
8._____
9._____
10._____
11._____
12._____
13._____
14._____
15._____
16._____
17._____
18._____
19._____
20._____
21._____
22._____
23._____
24._____
25._____

Go get a friend asshole. Then play the damn game. Players take turns initialing each cunt circle, starting with the bottom row, but players can then place the damn discs anywhere as long as the spaces under them are filled. The winner is the player who gets four discs in a vertical, horizontal or diagonal row.

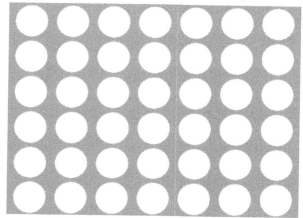

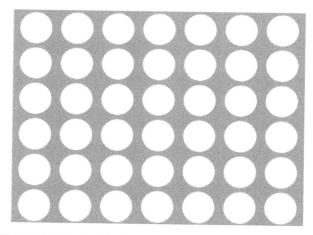

Hope your friend is still around for this fucker. One player is squares the other is circles. Each player takes turns drawing a horizontal or vertical line between two of their shapes. The goal is to be the first to create a single continuous line from one edge of the grid to the other (7-units). You cannot draw one line across another, so blocking the others move can be an advantage.

Connect the dots from 100 to 145
Don't let the extra numbers fuck your shit up!

230 248 278 240 276
258
218 268 233 249 245 242 244 243
247
233
146 264 101 253
223 168 238
246 102 245 100 250
238 254 226 274
257 237 272 237
254 110
254 103 255 255 111
251 109 236 224 236
270 279 108 107 116 112 166 239
271 264 185
104 248
265 230 258 113 167 249
262 106 115
250 105 114
256 238 269 212 259 169 265
241 239 257 272
259 242 241 214 171 247 243 266
262 196 195 239 210 269 267
244 239 253
117 119 118 172 198 241
202 239 262 173 170 268 260
237 275 222 123 124
237 236 259 226 261 250 245 206
236 256
268 225 271 174 263
235 211 239 229 122
217 212 210 275 188 263
246 266 277 125 236
235 243 238 236 120 209 121 126 238 175 176
234 279 215 207 213 271 278 261 248 178 240
197 265 238 214 276 199 269 187 177
273 189 260 186 182 180
127 132 134 133 140 143
260 228 200 183 213
263 278 217 264 179 215 275 194
252 129 266 130 256 135 136 201 218 273
137
270 277 220 261 216 231 181 209 267 237 249
251 279 276 227 247 270 208 274 246 252 193
128 131 138 139 141 142 144 145
184 228 252 237 190 192 274 251
234 224 204 244 242 225 227 191 220 211
272 257 267 216 229 273 255 205 231
253

Answer on page 105

Are you a bigot? Then you can shove this shit up your Ass. How many damn dots can you find below?

Answer on page 105

Why do they keep giving us these fuckers to fill out?

Your task is to fill every empty cell with a positive or negative integer in such a way so that each white cell's value equals the sum of its adjoining half-height cells. When complete, each Balance Quest puzzle grid will "balance" itself in such a way so that the four center cells surrounding the center "zero cell" will always add up to zero.

There are five rules that must be followed in every Quest puzzle:
The gray cells must include all integers between -16 and 16, except 0
No number can be repeated within any of the gray cells.
The number in each white cell must equal the sum of its adjoining cells. The center Zero cell is always the sum of all four adjacent cells.

** Numbers can (and will) be reused across both white and gray cells. The rules specify only that the -16 to 16 numbers can never be used more than once in the gray cells. Example is below:

-8		-8+6=-2
	-2	-1+5=4
6		
5		
	4	
-1		

-2	
	2
4	

-2+4=-2	
2	
	0
-9	

	-1	2+-9+
		-1+8=0
8		

-12						-21		-3
1	13						-3	5
-6		2						11
	15			0			2	4
2	15	18					-10	
-5			13		-7			9
-10	-3							-9
14						-2	1	-14

Answer on page 106

Don't text and drive asshole. Draw the squares.

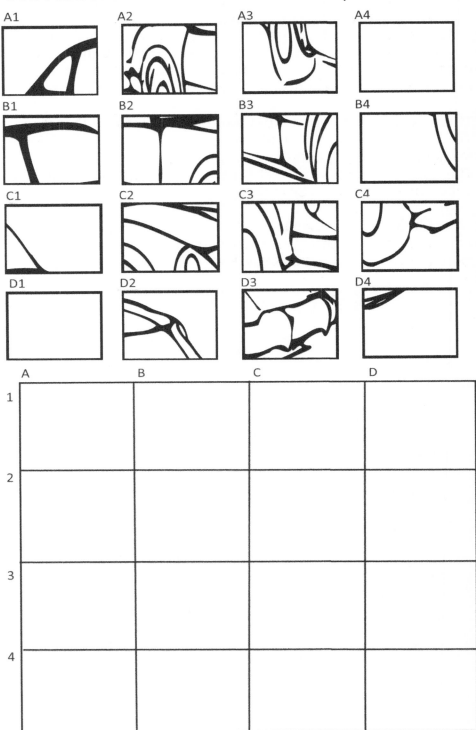

Image on page 106

Does anybody really like Sudoku? I bet that's a fuck no.

Numbers from 1 to 9 are inserted into sets that have 9 x 9 = 81 squares in whole. Every number can be used just once in e-furry, 3x3 block, column and row.

- Every number can be used just an once in the blocks of 3 x 3 = 9 square blocks. Got it? Good!
- Each row of 9 numbers ought to contain all digits 1 through 9 in any order. Is this shit clear?
- Every column of 9 numbers should comprise all digits 1 through 9 in any order. Have I lost your ass yet?

One way to figure out which numbers can go in each space is to use "process of elimination" by checking to see which other numbers are already included within each square – since there can be no duplication of numbers 1-9 within each square (or row or column).

7		1			9		3	
	2		7				6	5
				4				
		8			1		9	6
	9		3		8		4	
1	3		9			7		
				8				
3	1				6		7	
	8		5			4		9

Answer on page 106

This guy looks old as fuck! Find the 12 fucking hats hidden in image.

Answer on page 106

Now your ass can feel like a kid again!
Start at the top and work your way to the bottom

Answer on page 106

Can you stop damn talking while I'm trying to watch the movie in a theater! Draw the other half then color.

Why the hell would you want to do any math after school? But go ahead knock yourself out. I'm out.

For this problem use only the numbers 1, 2, 3, and 4 to solve. The numbers in each heavily outlined set of squares, called cages, must combine (in any order) to produce the damn target number in the top corner using the mathematical operation indicated (+, -, ×, ÷). This is almost too fucking much for me to explain. I need a break. OK, now use each number only once per row, once per column. Cages with just one square should be filled in with the target number in the top corner. A number can be repeated within a cage as long as it is not in the same row or column. I'm so glad that shit is done. Now get to filling this in so you can procrastinate the day away.

1-	4x		6x
	1	7+	
4÷	6x		
		2-	

Answer on page 106

I am so tired of explaining this shit to you, but here it is again. You are given a piece of text where each letter is substituted with a number and you need to decide which letters in the alphabet are being coded by the damn numbers you are given. The same fucking example is shown here:

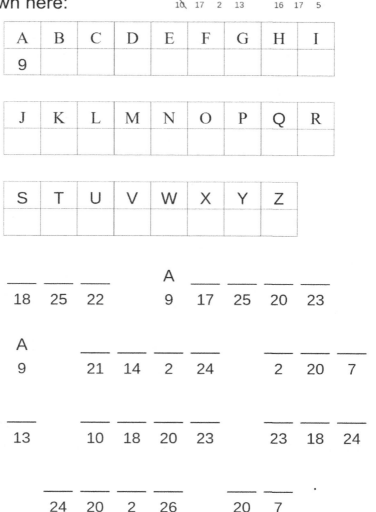

A	B	C	D	E	F	G	H	I	J	K	L	M
		2			16		13	9				10

N	O	P	Q	R	S	T	U	V	W	X	Y	Z
5	1				22	3	17					

T H i S   i S   S O
3 13 9 22   9 22   22 1

m U C H?. F U N .
10 17 2 13   16 17 5

A	B	C	D	E	F	G	H	I
9								

J	K	L	M	N	O	P	Q	R

S	T	U	V	W	X	Y	Z

___ ___ ___   A ___ ___ ___ ___
18 25 22   9 17 25 20 23

A ___ ___ ___ ___   ___ ___ ___
9   21 14 2 24   2 20 7

___ ___   ___ ___ ___ ___   ___ ___ ___
25 13   10 18 20 23   23 18 24

___ ___ ___ ___   ___ ___ .
24 20 2 26   20 7

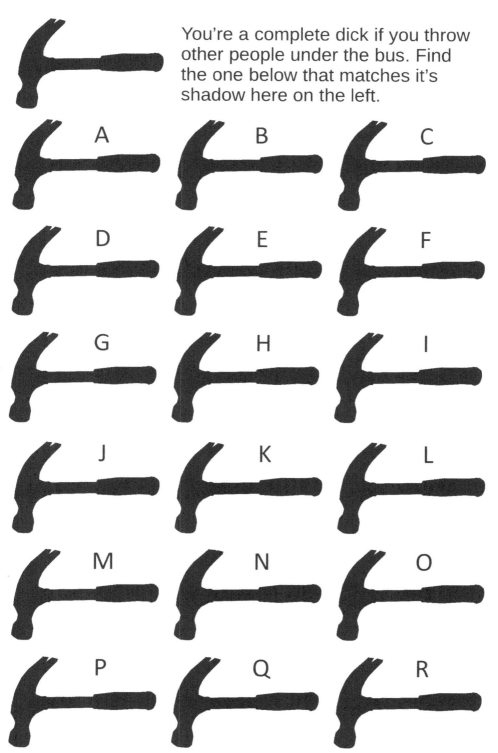

You're a complete dick if you throw other people under the bus. Find the one below that matches it's shadow here on the left.

Answer on page 106

61

I'm losing my shit trying to read this mess?

Move the tiles around to make the correct phrase.
The three letters on each tile must stay together
and in the given order. Tits to you for getting this far!

N N I	A R I	E T W	P R O	W A S
C O M	N D	A S	H T I	M I S
F I G	A	N G	S W E̶ Y	A
A W A	N G	E E N	R U	T E D
I N	N G .	V E N	E	B

S W E				

When you start off saying 'no offense' you are going to offend someone, just don't do it!

dickhead	dick	moron	douchebag
pollocks	shite	jackass	motherfucker
bullshit	manky	fuckwit	bitchtits

```
                  N  L  T  K
                  F  D  C  C
            M  J  I  V  X  Y
            S  D  S  R  Y  I
            H  O  L  U  C  F
            L  J  R  P  C  P
            C  K  H  O  S  V
            R  O  N  U  T  P
            H  B  N  G  P  E
            M  N  O  R  O  M
            V  M  W  S  Z  U
            M  H  I  O  S  W
            O  U  N  M  L  J
            T  E  S  Q  W  C
            H  V  B  S  U  V
            E  O  H  N  S  R
            R  N  T  K  L  O
            F  F  T  C  E  T
      C  E  T     U  L  J  M  L  O     F  D  N  X
      C  M  L  O  A  C  D  W  V  N  J  L  M  E  I  Y  I
   O  P  L     Z  Q  G  P  N  K  X  S  K  C  O  L  L  U  B  E  F
X  B  N  S  L  J  H  S  D  S  E  A  T  S  E  P  A  U  O  A  C  P
B  V  X  A  H  R  V  H  J  B  R  C  F  H  C  O  P  G  P  R  S  V
Y  E  C  M  F  I  N  B  W  H  P  C  B  L  R  W  X  X  G  A  O  P
P  F  H  O  S  R  T  I  A  H  F  S  V  U  H  J  K  L  O  D  P  F
V  P  I  N  L  O  S  E  W  S  U  O  P  R  L  O  P  P  T  O  Y  J
L  M  M  C  E  S  H  O  L  J  T  P  P  F  H  X  L  N  M  L  J  K  F
S  E  C  M  A  H  G  F  D  W  X  A  J  M  B  V  S  Q  W  R  N  U
Y  H  T  K  Y  N  O  B  C  H  E  E  G  E  Y  T  E  H  X  V  A  G
F  T  C  T  P  O  P  R  W  X  P  A  U  D  P  F  H  X  I  R  M  L     R  Y
U  A  L  J  G  U  F  H  J  K  B  O  G  F  O  P  M  J  H  T  W  U  V  O  D
J  E  D  W  X  G  L  M  B  E  R  J  L  M  I  Y  I  F  H  K  E  S  M  I  U
L  R  E  W  S  Z  S  L  H  T  H  O  U  S  E  F  T  U  T  C  Y  S  C  N  D
U  B  X  I  O  S  W  C  O  M  N  O  S  M  P  U  B  C  A  P  C  K  O  U  T
G  Z  O  P  U  R  U  D  N  L  T  I  W  K  C  U  F  B  O  P  H  C  X  A  O
C  Z  E  O  P  O  N  G  F  D  R  C  O  I  U  T  R  W  B  E  I  S  O  P  L
S  I  P  L  D  Z  Q  G  J  T  V  X  Y  M  P  O  D  I  A  R  E  X  B  N
X  A  I  T  S  O  H  F  I  S  R  Y  I  J  N  C  O  D  A  E  N  B  V
   V  X  Q  B  I  T  C  H  T  I  T  S  H  J  K  M  M  F  H  I  Y
      S  X  V  T  M  J  H  P  C  P  L  N  B  P  V  P  I  O
```

Answer on page 107

Clean up after yourself, bitch! Color this shit.

SON OF A BITCH

Who the hell fucked this shit up.
I'm gonna need your ass to unscramble this shit.

1. tHhao lsslblyi   _____

2. ihkb scc tuofeFf   _____

3. kgsi dB cfao   _____

4. ukgytrh Feneciv   _____

5. Wescis rdepki   _____

6. fcGu okt hup ewr   _____

7. dSuup iaf onrkgncto_____

8. ate'eb rurs aYod   _____

9. va ud ngc'lo ietc kuIf   _____

10. rokY aweun   _____

11. isth tEa   _____

12. wBe mol   _____

Answer on page 107

This a jackass puzzle where all the letters have for some goddamn reason fallen to the bottom, lazy assholes. They got then got fucking mixed up on their way down, idiots, but remain in the same row. Complete the puzzle by filling the letters into the column they fall under. You start by filling in the one-letter columns, because that shit doesn't have anywhere else to go in their column. Also try filling in common one-, two- and three-letter words as shown in the wicked tits example below.

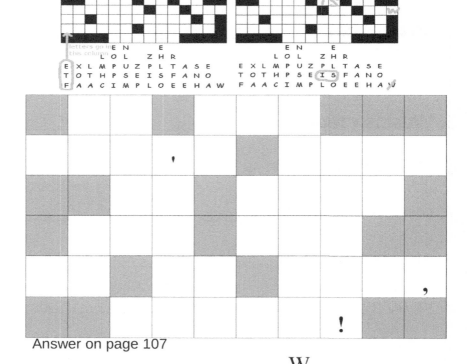

Answer on page 107

W

F　　　　　　　H

G　M　T　T　T　U　T

O　N　I　Y　O　U　E　N

O　F　E　M　T　O　L　A　K

D　I　B　E　Y　C　H　I　Y　E

Find the 12 differences between these fucked up desks.

Answer on page 107

How can these numbers still be messed up as fuck?

Try to fill in some more damn missing numbers. Who the shit keeps losing these fuckers anyway.

The missing numbers are integers from 1 and 9.
The numbers in each row add up to totals to the right.
The numbers in each column add up to the totals along the bottom. You know the goddamn drill by now!
The diagonal lines also add up the totals to the right.

					22
7		9		5	31
	8		1	7	21
5		7	2		19
	6	5		9	31
3	4		9		19
26	25	24	19	27	27

Answer on page 107

Why the hell am I supposed to do with this shit?

The figures given on the side and in top of the grid indicate the numbers of black boxes in that line or column.

For example 3,3 on the left of a line indicates that there is, from left to right, a block of 3 damn black boxes then a second block of 3 black boxes on the same crap line. To solve a puzzle, one needs to determine which cells will be boxes and which will be empty. Determining which cells are to be left empty is as important as those to be filled.

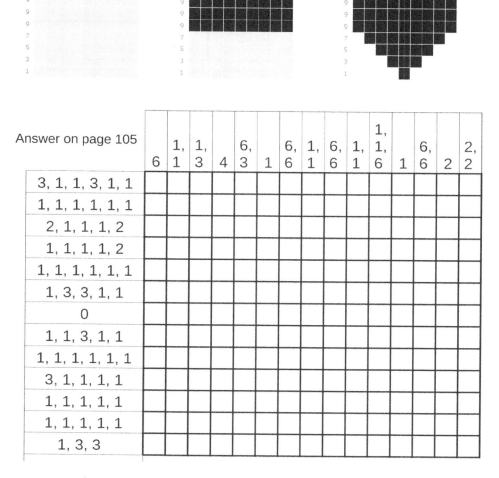

Answer on page 105

	6	1, 1	1, 3	4	6, 3	1	6, 6	1, 1	6, 6	1, 1	1, 1, 6	1	6, 6	2	2, 2
3, 1, 1, 3, 1, 1															
1, 1, 1, 1, 1, 1															
2, 1, 1, 1, 2															
1, 1, 1, 1, 2															
1, 1, 1, 1, 1, 1															
1, 3, 3, 1, 1															
0															
1, 1, 3, 1, 1															
1, 1, 1, 1, 1, 1															
3, 1, 1, 1, 1															
1, 1, 1, 1, 1															
1, 1, 1, 1, 1															
1, 3, 3															

Answer on page 107

I can't mentally handle this messed up shit anymore. Fit the numbered bricks into the square of bricks without changing their shape or breaking them up.

Answer on page 108

Math Squares

Oh my god! Look at this fucked up mess of a puzzle. Good fucking luck trying to fill in the missing numbers.

Use the numbers 1 through 9 to complete the equations.

Each row is a math equation. Work your way from left to right. Can anyone figure this shit out?
Each column is a math equation. Work from top to bottom. I'm out and maybe you should be too!

Fucking Hell! None of us want to hear you whistle. NO ONE!

3	x		-	1	/			2
+		x		x		x		
	-	4	x		+	6		46
-		+		-		/		
9	+		x	5	+			77
x		/		-		x		
	x	2	+		/	1		20
24		13		-1		21		

Answer on page 108

Make sure you stuff your face while you figure this shit out. Which one of these fuckers is different?

Answer on page 108

How many words can you find within the words:

Fuck that shit up

1. _____
2. _____
3. _____
4. _____
5. _____
6. _____
7. _____
8. _____
9. _____
10. _____
11. _____
12. _____
13. _____
14. _____
15. _____
16. _____
17. _____
18. _____
19. _____
20. _____
21. _____
22. _____
23. _____
24. _____
25. _____

Go get your smartass friend again, you can't do this shit alone.
Take turns drawing lines between two adjacent dots with a horizontal
or vertical line. The play who completes the fourth side of the box,
initials the box and gets to draw another line. When all the boxes are
completed the winner is the player who has initialed the most boxes.

Each player takes a turn writing an 'S' or 'O' in a square. The goal is to complete the damn sequence S-O-S in three adjacent squares (vertical, horizontal, diagonal). When a player completes the shitty sequence, they mark it as theirs. Play continues until all squares are occupied. Player with the most wins. Don't be a sore fucking loser!

Go get some goddamn coffee, your're going to need it!

The figures given on the side and in top of the grid show the damn numbers of black boxes in that line or column.

For fucks sake it's simple, 3,3 on the left of a line indicates that there is, from left to right, a block of 3 black boxes then a second block of 3 black boxes on the same line. To solve a puzzle, one needs to determine which cells will be boxes and which will be empty. Determining which cells are to be left empty is as important as those to be filled.

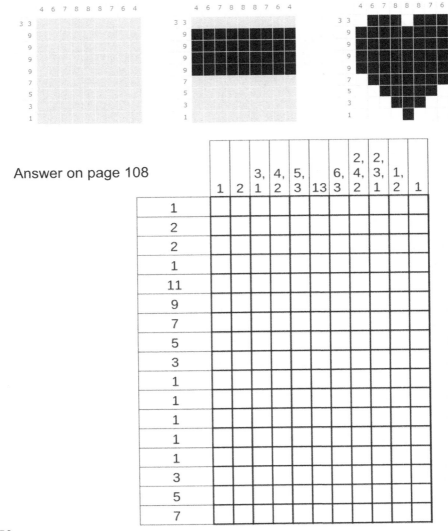

Answer on page 108

Fucking Hell who put this fucking Sudoku in here again!!!

Numbers from 1 to 9 are inserted into sets that have 9 x 9 = 81 squares in whole. Every shit number can be used just once in every damn 3x3 block, column and row.

- Every number can be used just once in the blocks of 3 x 3 = 9 square blocks. JUST ONCE, dammit!
- Each row of 9 numbers ought to contain all digits 1 through 9 in any order. Don't leave any fucker out.
- Every column of 9 numbers should comprise all digits 1 through 9 in any order. Good fucking luck!

One way to figure out which numbers can go in each space is to use "process of elimination" by checking to see which other numbers are already included within each square – since there can be no duplication of numbers 1-9 within each square (or row or column).

9	6			4		1		
			3	8				
7		8		6				9
1	2		8			9		3
				5				
3		5			2		6	4
8				9		4		7
				3	8			
		9		2			8	5

Answer on page 108

My lazy ass is done with these fucking messed up words! Unscramble the shit phrases.

1. uph ktS cuu tehf   _____

2. ehe aWt htllh   _____

3. fn isrio atShbr   _____

4. tgcng bniyuDa   _____

5. osaK msey shisl   _____

6. fleytSs urioh   _____

7. tukS ucbc ipht   _____

8. kck oFer fusas   _____

9. rShf rstiai nob   _____

10. mue cFk   _____

11. Hkyu reefc   _____

12. itpw dScuo   _____

Answer on page 108

Fuck me sideways, these fuckers keep getting bigger and bigger. How are you going to fill in the missing numbers this time? You're fucking on your own here.

The missing numbers are integers from 1 to 9.
The numbers in each row add up to totals to the right.
The numbers in each column add up to the totals along the bottom. So many fucking numbers.
The diagonal lines also add up the totals to the right.

						39
	5	4		9	7	33
9			8	3	1	30
2	1	5		8		27
5		6	3		1	24
4	7		9	6		35
	3	8	4		5	31
31	24	27	37	35	26	27

Answer on page 108

Don't blame others for your faults

Your task is to fill every empty cell with a positive or negative integer in such a way so that each white cell's value equals the sum of its adjoining half-height cells. When complete, each Balance Quest puzzle grid will "balance" itself in such a way so that the four center cells surrounding the center "zero cell" will always add up to zero.

There are five rules that must be followed in every Quest puzzle
The gray cells must include all integers between -16 and 16, except
No number can be repeated within any of the gray cells. SHIT NO!
The number in each white cell must equal the sum of its adjoining cells. The center Zero cell is always the sum of all four adjacent cells

** Numbers can (and will) be reused across both white and gray cells
The rules specify only that the -16 to 16 numbers can never be used more than once in the gray cells. The same damn example is below:

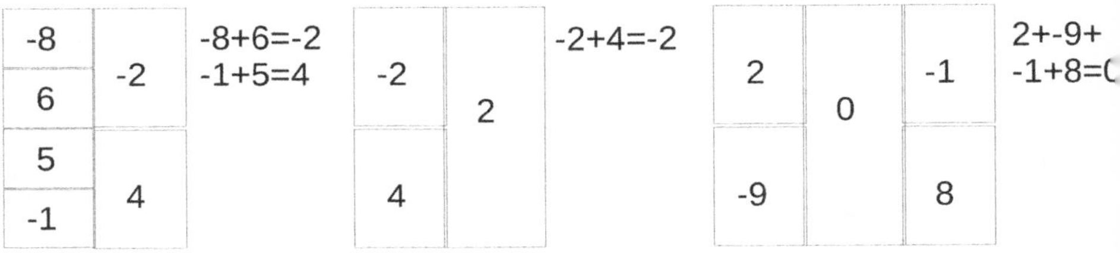

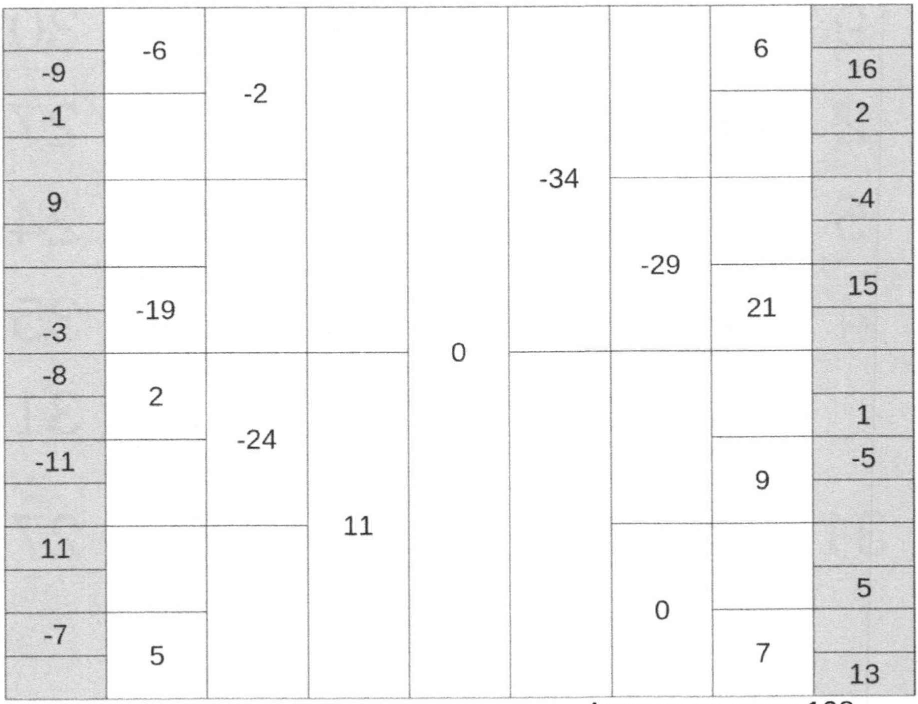

-8		-8+6=-2			-2+4=-2					2+-9+
6	-2	-1+5=4	-2			2		-1		-1+8=C
5				2			0			
-1	4		4			-9		8		

Puzzle grid values:

-9	-6						6		16
-1		-2							2
					-34				
9									-4
						-29			15
-3	-19						21		
-8				0					
	2								1
-11		-24						9	-5
			11						
11									5
						0		7	
-7	5								13

Answer on page 108

Your a huge dick if you park too close to the line.
Figure out how to fit the bricks into the square without
changing their shape or breaking them into pieces.

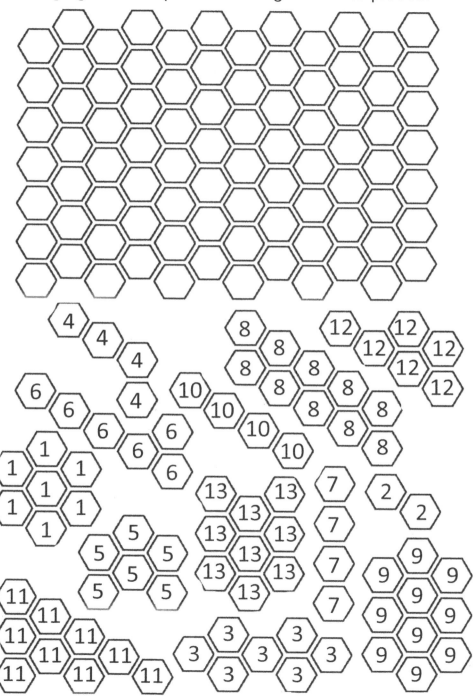

Answer on page 108

Who the fuck doesn't love a damn maze!
Start at the top and work your way to the bottom

Answer on page 109

Even a drunk fucker can figure this shit out. Find the 13 fucking bottles hidden in image.

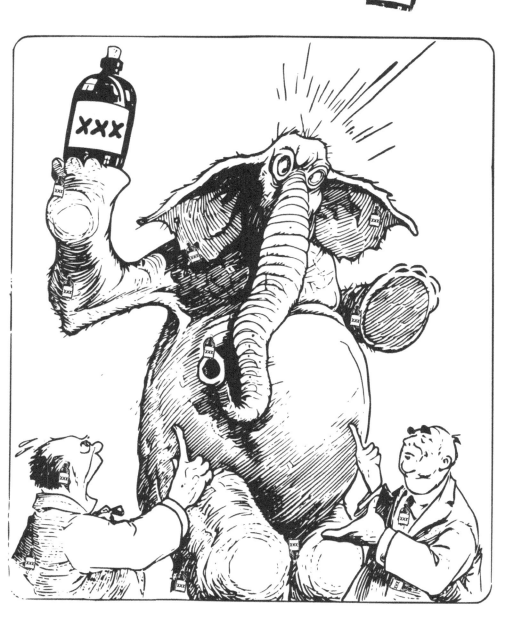

Answer on page 109

This a jackass puzzle where all the letters have for some goddamn reason fallen to the bottom, lazy assholes. They got then got fucking mixed up on their way down, idiots, but remain in the same row. Complete the puzzle by filling the letters into the column they fall under. You start by filling in the one-letter columns, because that shit doesn't have anywhere else to go in their column. Also try filling in common one-, two- and three-letter words as shown in the wicked tits example below.

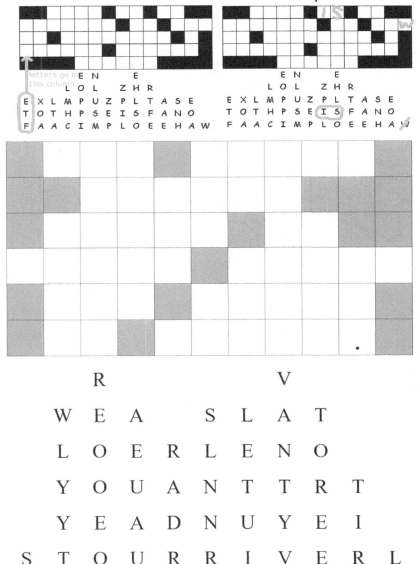

These lines are fucked. Color this shit.

Connect the dots from 100 to 141
Don't let the extra numbers fool your ass!

258 268 230 278 240 276
218 246 233 248 249 244 243
245
238 246 223 118 119 122 123 242 238
146 145 117 245 247 250 124 237
243
257 274 236
251 254 279 120 121 275 239
270 116 254 254 185 237 125
271 262 230 226 255 168
256 115 161 144 264 248 253 236 169 167 249
258 126
264 238 114 241 250 259 257 127 272 265
259 113 212 128 265
233 239 242 241 214 171 210 207 266
244 239 129 269
143 239 253 111 112 262 130 170 267
247 255 131 241
237 236 110 222 243 195 250 268 260
236 147 259 109 261 132
268 225 256 271 174 245 263
142 235 148 212 211 277 196 265
107 108 197 275 133 134 238 188 263
235 217 266 198 173 135 175 176 240
239 210 209 248
152 279 106 278 136 187 178 177
269 272 215 105 271 261 186 182 179
239 151 214 213 189 137 138 180
234 166 238 104 276 184 183
103 226 206
260 228 278 217 264 218 139 273 275 194 213
263 266 273 102 199 231 140 209 267 237 249
153 277 220 256 101 215 270 181 274 246 252 193
270 237 279 200 227 247 229 208 224 202 274 252
262 242 224
164 260 236 238 237 228 225 190 229 192 211 251
234 224 252 172 244 141 227 191 231 220
100
272 276 257 204 216 236 258 255 205
267 251 216 201 269 253 273

Answer on page 109

Stop being an ass to servers. Draw the squares.

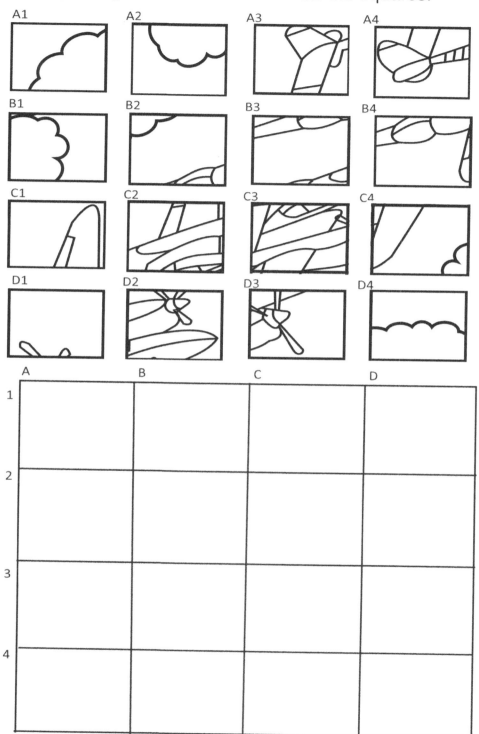

Which one of these assholes is different from the rest?

Image on page 109

Math Squares

Fucking hell. Look at this fucked up mess of a puzzle.
Good fucking luck trying to fill in the missing numbers.

Use the numbers 1 through 9 to complete the equations.

Each row is a math equation. Work your way from left to right. Can anyone figure this shit out?
Each column is a math equation. Work from top to bottom. I'm out and maybe you should be too!

Fucking Hell! I'm out and tired of this shit.

	/	4	-		x	6	-18
+		x		+		/	
9	-		/	1	+		5
-		+		x		-	
	+	2	-		+	7	3
x		/		-		x	
5	x		+	1	/		2
75		10		47		-40	

Image on page 109

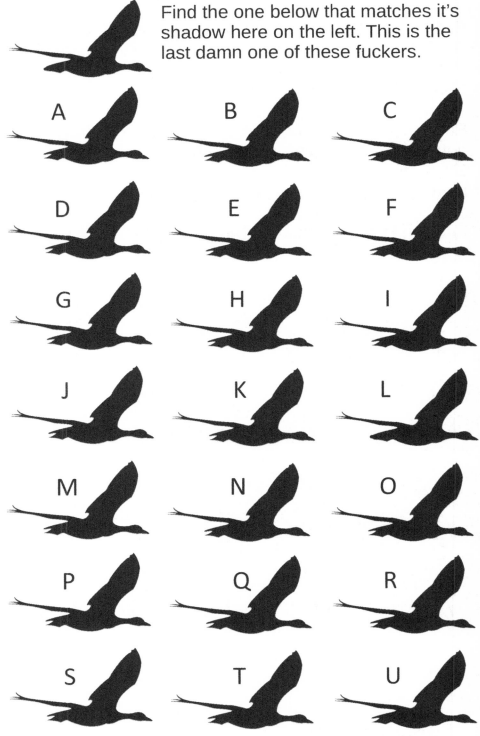

Find the one below that matches it's shadow here on the left. This is the last damn one of these fuckers.

A

B

C

D

E

F

G

H

I

J

K

L

M

N

O

P

Q

R

S

T

U

Answer on page 109

Cryptogram

Answer on page 109

I don't want to talk abot this sit again, but here it is. You are given a piece of text where each letter is substituted with a number and you need to decide which letters in the alphabet are being coded by the damn numbers you are given. The same fucking example is shown here:

A	B	C	D	E	F	G	H	I	J	K	L	M
		2			16		13	9				10

N	O	P	Q	R	S	T	U	V	W	X	Y	Z
5	1				22	3	17					

T H I S   I S   S O
3 13 9 22   9 22   22 1

M U C H?   F U N .
10 17 2 13   16 17 5

A	B	C	D	E	F	G	H	I

J	K	L	M	N	O	P	Q	R

S	T	U	V	W	X	Y	Z
9							

___   ___ ___ S ___   ___ ___ ___ ___
21   2 14 9 26   24 3 18 19

___ ___ ___ '   ___ ___   ___ ___ ___ ___ ___
20 18 14   4 23   17 18 21 3 17

___ ___   ___ ___ ___ ___   ___ ___ ___ S
26 18   6 14 1 24   26 11 21 9

S ___ ___ ___   ___ ___ .
9 11 21 26   14 12

I hope your eyes are fucking working. How many damn shapes can you find below?

Answer on page 109

These fucking words decided to get lost in this shit.
So now you have to find those assholes.

fuck	dammit	jerk	bitch
sissy	bastard	cunt	asshole
idiot	balls	swine	dumbass

```
                    P  U  A  E  D  N  L  T  G  W  P  I  D
                 E  O  L  L  N  G  F  D  H  P  L  M  M  T  E
              O  P  N  F  Z  Q  D  R  A  T  S  A  B  A  N  D  N
           X  B  T  M  L  A  H  F  D  S  T  U  R  D  J  C  E  I  Y
        N  B  O  X  Q  S  L  R  R  G  H  P  G  E  I  O  K  M  I  P  F
     O  I  I  E  R  R  A  V  P  R  J  H  F  K  S  O  Y  B  P  Q  W  P  I
  B  W  D  P  F              I  O  T  R  S                 A  L  M  M  C
  I  I  Q  V  P              T  W  E  G  O                 R  G  E  C  M
  A  P  P  L  M              O  J  S  D  P                 Y  H  R  J  V
  P  U  R  S  E              F  K  D  U  J                 X  C  I  E  M
  P  I  Y  R  D              M  E  T  N  Z                 E  T  O  Y  V
  B  C  X  E  I              V  O  D  R  S                 E  I  B  S  M
  P  O  I  Y  T  E  L  D  Z  Q  G  J  N  I  N  J  H  F  D  M  N  B  V  T  Q
  O  E  E  X  B  N  F  D  J  H  F           L  A  V  M  M  C  I  Y  T  I  S
  O  L  N  B  V  X  Q  U  R  V  H           X  V  P  S  E  N  O  J  O  C  X
  Q  O  I  Y  T  A  R  O  C  P  M           S  R  Y  S  S  I  S  V  P  K  K
  B  H  O  P  F  H  X  R  R  K  I           L  O  F  J  W  N  L  L  M  E  C
  I  S  Q  V  P  I  K  L  O  F  T  W  T  C  E  T  C  H  C  O  D  L  V  N  J
  A  S  P              E  T  U  O  L  J  B  A  L  L  S  R  W        I  I  J
  M  A  R  S              O  G  A  R  U  S  A  B  L           I  J  W  N
  S  R  P  L  D              N  V  X  Y  M  H  J  K           F  H  S  O
  A  B  M  M  L  J                                      C  P  L  R  D
  B  T  X  J  W  R                                   F  S  G  C  U  J
  Y  T  U  S  M  V  P                             G  J  G  I  M  S  O
  P  F  H  P  S  T  Y  I                       L  O  W  P  B  H  X  B
  V  P  I  K  E  N  F  T  W  T  U  O  P  R  S  O  P  P  T  O  A  O  M  B  V
     M  M  C  E  U  J  P  L  J  G  P  F  H  X  B  N  K  T  S  P  T  T  Y
        C  M  L  C  M  F  D  W  X  G  J  O  B  V  X  E  S  R  T  U  O
           H  F  S  V  I  O  T  I  M  M  A  D  T  E  S  X  O  O  G
              U  O  P  R  H  X  P  T  U  A  P  F  H  X  S  R  C
                 P  F  H  J  K  E  N  W  R  S  T  O  J  H  X
                    J  M  B  F  R  J  L  M  R  Y  I  K  H
```

Answer on page 110

Who keeps messing up these fucked up tiles?

Move the tiles around to make the correct phrase.
The three letters on each tile must stay together
and in the given order. Tits to you for getting this far!

O N '	K S T	I A R	E ,		E A R
E N S	D O	I D		F U	S A
I N G	I V E	B A C	S I V		F I N
O F F	I N D	N G		I	T F
E R S	D L	B U T	F E N		A B B
O F	C K I	S W	N D		

I D				

Answer on page 110

Draw the other half of this shit then add your own crap.

Find the 13 differences between the screwed up mess.

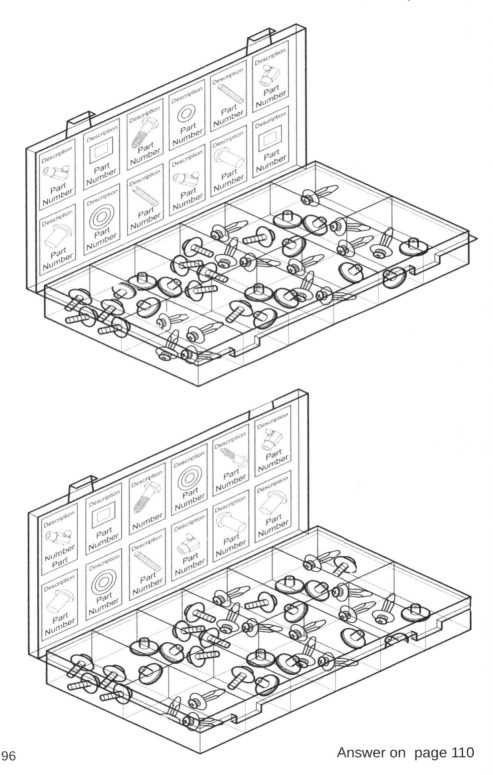

Answer on page 110

Why the hell would you want to do any of this hard shit?

For this problem use only the numbers 1, 2, 3, 4and 5 to solve. The numbers in each heavily outlined set of squares, called cages, must combine (in any order) to produce the damn target number in the top corner using the mathematical operation indicated (+, -, ×, ÷). This is almost too fucking much for me to explain. I need a break. OK, now use each number only once per row, once per column. Cages with just one square should be filled in with the target number in the top corner. A number can be repeated within a cage as long as it is not in the same row or column. I'm so glad that shit is done. Now get to filling this in so you can procrastinate the day away.

9+		3-	12x	
4+				3-
	2÷	10+		
1-		6x		7+
	5			

Answer on page 110

How many words can you find within the words:

Holy Shitballs is Right!

1. _____
2. _____
3. _____
4. _____
5. _____
6. _____
7. _____
8. _____
9. _____
10. _____
11. _____
12. _____
13. _____
14. _____
15. _____
16. _____
17. _____
18. _____
19. _____
20. _____
21. _____
22. _____
23. _____
24. _____
25. _____

You need a fucking friend for this shit. Good luck finding one!
Each player takes a turn picking a word to spell out and draws lines
underneath to represent the letters in the word. The other person
guesses letters. Any letters that fit in the word, get put into the word.
The other letters are placed on top above the image and parts of a
stick man are drawn till the word is guessed or stick man is well hung.

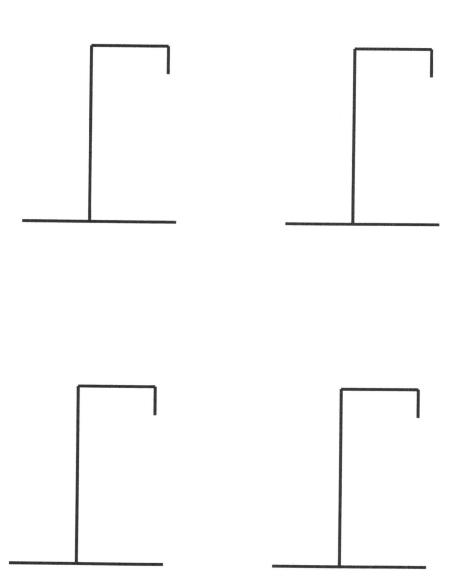

Players alternately join the fucking dots on a hexagon by drawing along the lines provided; the first player who is forced to complete a triangle in their own color loses. So don't lose, bitch!

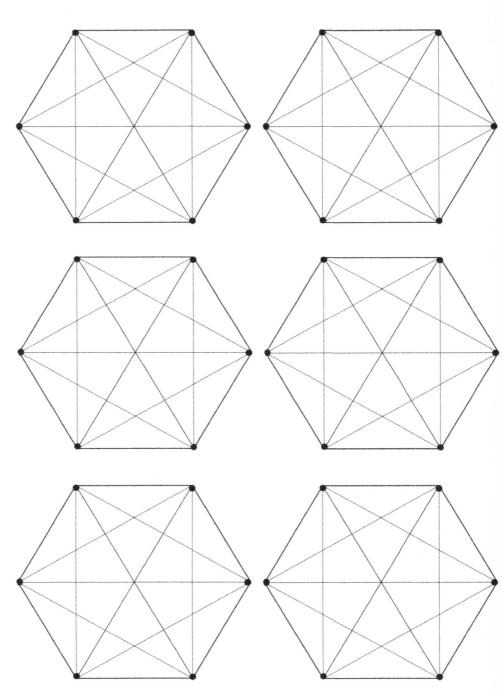

Page 1

Page 2

Page 3

Page 4

I tried really hard to stop swearing but I just cunt.

9	/	3	+	4	7
-		x		/	
7	-	8	x	2	-2
+		/		+	
5	-	6	x	1	-1
7		4		3	

Page 5

Page 7

1	1	1	4	4	4
3	1	3	6	4	4
3	3	3	6	6	6
2	7	7	8	8	8
2	2	7	5	5	5
2	2	2	5	5	5

Page 8

I'm classy as fuck, but I cuss a little.

Page 9

Page 10

	1, 4, 1	1, 1, 4	0	7	1	7	0	1, 1	1, 7, 1	0	1	7	1
3, 1, 1, 3, 3													
1, 1, 1, 1, 1													
1, 1, 1, 1, 1													
3, 3, 1, 1													
1, 1, 1, 1, 1													
1, 1, 1, 1, 1													
3, 1, 1, 3, 1													

101

Page 11

Page 12

				26
3	1	6	5	15
4	2	9	8	23
8	7	3	2	20
5	4	1	7	17
20	14	19	22	15

1. Fucking shit
2. Son of a bitch
3. Fucking great
4. Crotch face
5. Fuck my life
6. Worthless cock
7. Buzz off bitchtits
8. You suck ass
9. Lazy piece of shit
10.,Piss off
11. Go to hell
12. Up yours

Page 13

Page 14

My swear jar could finance the fucking space program.

Page 15

Page 16

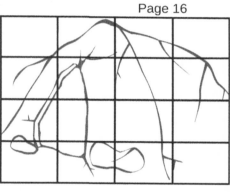

Page 17

O

102

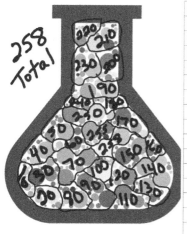

258 Total

12	4						4	11
-8		-2				-4		-7
13	14		-7				-8	-13
1					-33			5
-9	5						-4	10
14		-5				-29		-14
6	-10						3	-6
-16				0				9
-2	13						1	-3
15		5				-26		4
-10	-8		11				-27	-12
2					-24			-15
16	23						11	8
7		11				2		3
-11	-12						-9	-4
-1								-5

1	8	5	7	4	9	2	3	6
7	9	4	2	6	3	8	5	1
3	6	2	8	1	5	7	4	9
9	4	7	1	3	8	5	6	2
5	2	1	9	7	6	3	8	4
8	3	6	5	2	4	1	9	7
6	1	3	4	5	2	9	7	8
2	5	8	6	9	7	4	1	3
4	7	9	3	8	1	6	2	5

2-		2x
1	3	2
5+		
3	2	1
2	4+	
2	1	3

I really don't give two shits about you.

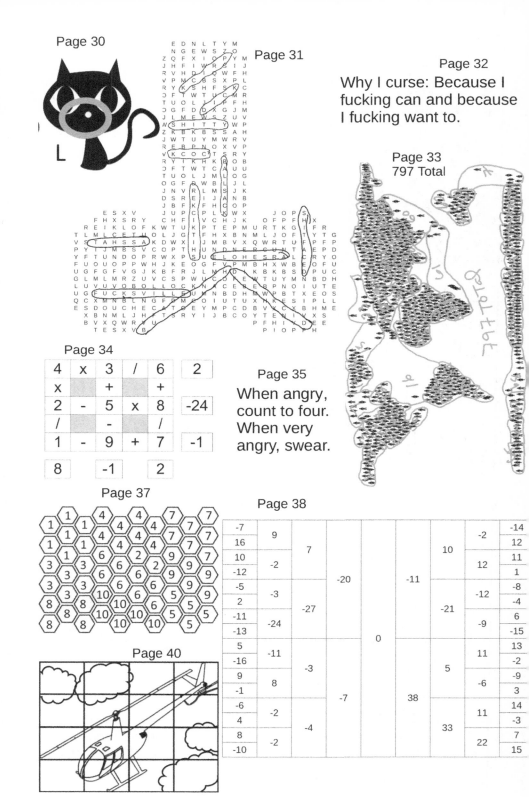

Page 30

L

Page 31

Page 32
Why I curse: Because I fucking can and because I fucking want to.

Page 33
797 Total

Page 34

4	x	3	/	6	2
x		+		+	
2	-	5	x	8	-24
/		-		/	
1	-	9	+	7	-1
8		-1		2	

Page 35
When angry, count to four. When very angry, swear.

Page 37

Page 38

-7	9				10	-2	-14
16		7					12
10	-2					12	11
-12			-20	-11			1
-5	-3				-21	-12	-8
2		-27					-4
-11	-24					-9	6
-13			0				-15
5	-11				5	11	13
-16		-3					-2
9	8			38		-6	-9
-1			-7				3
-6	-2				33	11	14
4		-4					-3
8	-2					22	7
-10							15

Page 40

Page 41

4	3	7	5	1	9	8	6	2
1	9	2	8	6	3	7	4	5
6	5	8	7	2	4	3	1	9
5	6	1	3	9	8	4	2	7
9	8	4	2	7	6	1	5	3
7	2	3	4	5	1	6	9	8
2	1	9	6	3	7	5	8	4
8	7	6	9	4	5	2	3	1
3	4	5	1	8	2	9	7	6

Page 42

(nonogram solution)

Column clues: 4,1,1 / 1,1,4 / 0 / 7 / 1 / 7 / 0 / 1,1 / 7 / 1 / 0 / 1 / 7 / 1

Row clues:
3, 1, 1, 3, 3
1, 1, 1, 1, 1
1, 1, 1, 1, 1
3, 3, 1
1, 1, 1, 1, 1
1, 1, 1, 1, 1
3, 1, 1, 3, 1

Page 44

1- 1	6x 3	2	9+ 4
2	4 4	4÷ 1	3
1- 3	2x 1	4	2
4	2	4+ 3	1

Page 45

					20
8	4	2	5	1	20
1	6	7	3	9	26
2	1	3	6	8	20
4	7	5	9	2	27
6	9	5	3	7	30
21	27	22	26	27	33

Page 47

1. What a bastard
2. Eat shit and die
3. Lick my cunt
4. Don't be a dick
5. Ass kisser
6. Bloody hell
7. Fuck this shit
8. Penis face
9. Suck my cock
10. Fuck yourself
11. Kiss my ass
12. Get lost jerk

Page 43

Page 46

Page 51

Page 52

354 Total

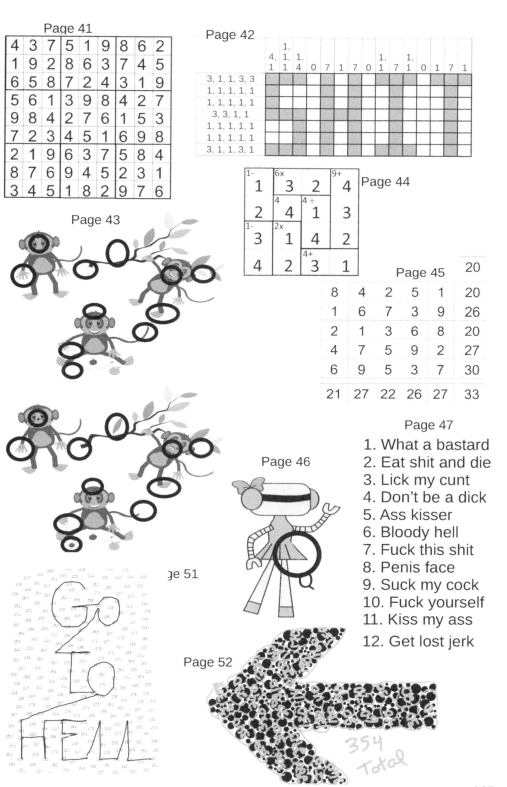

105

Page 53

-12	-23	-10	-8	0	2	-21	-18	-15
-11								-3
1	13						-3	5
12								-8
-7	-13	2				23	21	11
-6								10
16	15						2	-2
-1								4
2	15	18	13		-7	-5	-10	3
13								-13
8	3						5	9
-5								-4
-10	-3	-5				-2	-3	-9
7								6
14	-2						1	15
-16								-14

Page 54

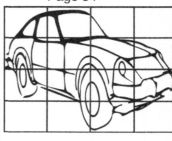

Page 55

7	5	1	6	2	9	8	3	4
8	2	4	7	1	3	9	6	5
9	6	3	8	4	5	1	2	7
5	4	8	2	7	1	3	9	6
2	9	7	3	6	8	5	4	1
1	3	6	9	5	4	7	8	2
4	7	9	1	8	2	6	5	3
3	1	5	4	9	6	2	7	8
6	8	2	5	3	7	4	1	9

Page 56

Page 57

Page 59

1- 3	4x 4	1	6x 2
2	1 1	7+ 4	3
4÷ 4	6x 2	3	1
1	3	2- 2	4

Page 60

How about a
nice cup of
shut the fuck up.

N

Page 61

Page 62

Swearing was invented as a compromise between running away and fighting.

Page 63

Page 65
1. Holy shitballs
2. Fuck off bitches
3. Bag of dicks
4. Fuck everything
5. Wicked pisser
6. Grow the fuck up
7. Stop fucking around
8. You're a basterd
9. I couldn't give a fuck
10. You wanker
11. Eat shit
12. Blow me

Page 66

If you don't like me then get out of my way, bitch!

Page 67

Page 68

7	6	9	4	5	31
3	8	2	1	7	21
5	1	7	2	4	19
8	6	5	3	9	31
3	4	1	9	2	19
26	25	24	19	27	27

22

Page 69

107

Page 70

8	8	8	5	5	5	5
8	8	3	3	3	1	1
8	7	7	3	1	1	1
2	7	7	4	4	9	9
2	2	4	4	4	4	9
6	2	6	10	10	10	11
6	6	6	10	10	10	11

Page 71

3	x	5	-	1	/	7	2
+		x		x		x	
9	-	4	x	8	+	6	46
-		+		-		/	
9	+	6	x	5	+	2	77
x		/		-		x	
8	x	2	+	4	/	1	20
24		13		-1		21	

Page 72

Page 76

Column clues: 1 | 2 | 3,1 | 4,2 | 5,3 | 13 | 6,3 | 2,4,2 | 2,3,1 | 1,2 | 1

Row clues: 1, 2, 2, 1, 11, 9, 7, 5, 3, 1, 1, 1, 1, 1, 3, 5, 7

Page 77

9	6	2	7	4	5	1	3	8
5	4	1	3	8	9	2	7	6
7	3	8	2	6	1	5	4	9
1	2	6	8	7	4	9	5	3
4	9	7	6	5	3	8	1	2
3	8	5	9	1	2	7	6	4
8	5	3	1	9	6	4	2	7
2	7	4	5	3	8	6	9	1
6	1	9	4	2	7	3	8	5

Page 78

1. Shut the fuck up
2. What the hell
3. Shit for brains
4. Dingy cuntbag
5. Kiss my asshole
6. Shit yourself
7. Stuck up bitch
8. For fucks sake
9. Shit for brains
10. Fuck me
11. Hey fucker
12. Stupid cow

Page 79

2	5	4	6	9	7	33
9	6	3	8	3	1	30
2	1	5	7	8	4	27
5	2	6	3	7	1	24
4	7	1	9	6	8	35
9	3	8	4	2	5	31
31	24	27	37	35	26	27

Page 80

Col 1	Col 2	Col 3	Col 4	Col 5	Col 6	Col 7	Col 8
3						6	-10
-9	-6				-5		16
-1		-2				-11	2
-2	-3		-4	-34			-13
9						3	-4
8	17			-29			7
-16		-2				21	15
-3	-19		0				6
-8						-13	-14
10	2				-4		1
-11		-24					-5
-15	-26		11	-4		9	14
11							-12
4	15				0	-7	5
-7		20					-6
12	5					7	13

Page 81

3	3	3	3	12	12	12	13	13
3	3	3	3	9	12	13	13	
7	1	1	9	9	9	12	13	13
7	1	1	9	9	6	13	13	13
7	1	1	9	9	8	8	6	6
7	10	4	9	11	8	8	8	6
7	5	10	4	4	11	8	8	6
5	5	10	11	11	8	8	8	
5	5	2	2	4	11	11	11	

Page 82

Page 83

Page 84
You never really learn to swear until you start to drive.

Page 86

Page 87

Page 88

H

Page 89

8	/	4	-	5	x	6	-18
+		x		+		/	
9	-	7	/	1	+	3	5
-		+		x		-	
2	+	2	-	8	+	7	3
x		/		-		x	
5	x	3	+	1	/	8	2
75		10		47		-40	

Page 90
L

Page 92

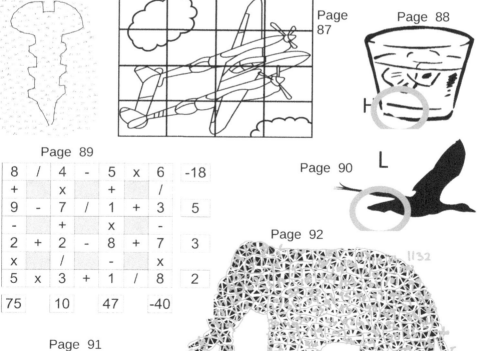

Page 91
I just know you're
going to fuck this shit up.

Page 93

Page 94

I don't find swearing offensive, but I do find liars and backastabbers fucking offensive.

Page 96

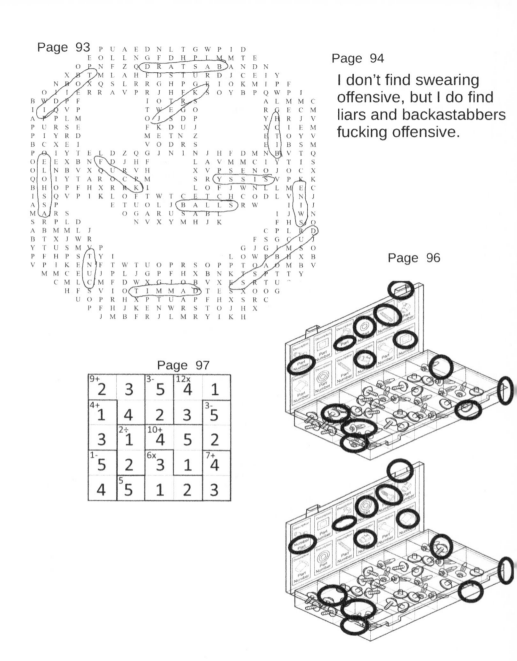

Page 97

9+ 2	3	3- 5	12x 4	1
4+ 1	4	2	3	3- 5
3	2÷ 1	10+ 4	5	2
1- 5	2	6x 3	1	7+ 4
4	5 5	1	2	3

Thank you for your damn purchase!!
I hope you found this shit fun as hell.
Please consider leaving a review.

http://www.amazon.com/T.L.-Adams/e/B00YSROGC4
tamaraadamsauthor@gmail.com

Books by Tamara L Adams

Mood Tracker Planner
Defiant (YA Dystopian Novel Series)
Art Up This Journal #1 and #2 Series
Backstabbing Bitches: Adult Activities
Puptivities: Adult Activities
Cativities: Adult Activities
Christmas Activities: Adult Activity Book/Bucket List
Activititties: Adult Activities
I Hate My Boss: Adult Activities
Activity Book for Adults
Activity Book You Never Knew You Wanted But Can't Live Without
Activity Book You need to Buy Before You Die
Fuck This Shit: Vulgar Activities
What an Asshole: Vulgar Activities
Fuck I'm Bored #1 and #2 Series : Adult Activity Book
I'm Still Fucking Bored: Adult Activity Book
The Activity Book That Will Transform Your Life
Activities to do while you number two
Unmotivated Coloring Quotes
Angry Coloring
Coloring Happy Quotes
Guided Bullet/Dot Planner
Coloring Cocktails
Cussing Creatures Color
100, 76 and 51 Quote Inspired Journal Prompts Series
Unlocking Happiness Planner
Cleaning and Organizing Planner
Daily Fitness Planner
Bloggers Daily Planner
Bloggers Daily Planner w margins
Writers Daily Planner
Busy Mothers Planner
Where's Woody Coloring Book
99 Writing Prompts
Deciding Destiny Series: Christy, Matt, Joe or Linsday
Rich Stryker Sreies: Julie's Last Hope/Tom's Final Justice
Unlocking Happiness
Getting to Know Yourself Journal and #2 Series
Timmy and the Dragon Children's Picture Book
Jacob and Ronnie the Robot Blast off to the Moon

Check out these other items by the Author:

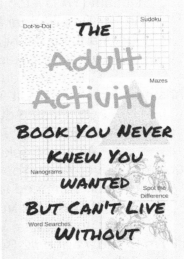

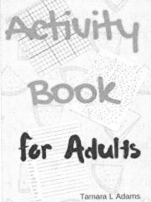

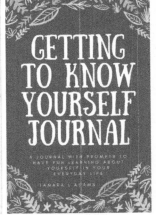

Other
Titles
By
The
Author

Thanks for your purchase!!

Please leave a review! I would be grateful.

Contact me to get a free printable PDF of Activities here at:

http://www.tamaraladamsauthor.com/free-printable-activity-book-pdf/

Tamaraadamsauthor@gmail.com

Thank you for your support and have a great day!

You can contact me at

http://www.amazon.com/T.L.-Adams/e/B00YSROGC4

Tammy@tamaraladamsauthor.com

https://www.pinterest.com/TamaraLAdamsAuthor/

https://twitter.com/TamaraLAdams

https://www.facebook.com/TamaraLAdamsAuthor/

https://www.youtube.com/user/tamaraladams

https://www.instagram.com/tamaraladamsauthor/

http://www.tamaraladamsauthor.com

All Cartoon Drawings are from https://publicdomainvectors.org

Made in the USA
Las Vegas, NV
20 November 2023

81228319R00069